Photography In Me
Beien Lin

Table of Contents

Dedication

I would like to dedicate this book to my parents. They have been with me through thick and thin. They would encourage me when I failed at something. They taught me how to stand up on my own when I fell down. My parents were the ones who got me the first camera after seeing how much I love photography. I am really thankful to have them as my parents.

Acknowledgment

I would like to thank many people for helping me complete this book. First of all, I would like to thank my teacher Shanette Carpenter for helping me and guiding me. Without your encouragement and support, I would not be able to publish this book. I would like to thank my friends especially Lisa for not getting upset with all my questions. Most importantly I would like to thank my family for be there and helping me along the way.

Background Information On Photography

You probably have heard the word "photography" your entire life. Have you wondered where this word came from? Photography is a Greek based word. In Greek the word Photo means lights. The second part of the word *-graphy* comes from the Greek word graphein, which means to draw. Photography is using light to create a picture that can be captured in an instant.

Joseph Nicephore Niepce took the first photograph in 1827. Niepce's first photograph took eight hours of light exposure to be created; however, the picture didn't last very long. Louis Daguerre partnered with Niepce in 1829 to work together to improve Niepce's process. After Niepce's death, in 1839, Daguerre created The Daguerreotype. The Daguerreotype only took a few minutes to develop and it would not change when exposed to light. In 1850, there were more than seventy Daguerreotype studios that were opened in New York City alone.

Henry Fox Talbot made the first negatives of a picture. He was a scientist that studies plants and a mathematician. Talbot moistened a paper with a silver salt solution and exposed it to light. Then the background became black and the picture became shades of gray. Then he reversed the lighting of the picture to create the photo. In 1841, he successfully perfected this method of turning the negative into the positive picture.

Hand held cameras were introduced in 1879. Then about ten years later, flexile roll films was created. George Eastman created the roll films.

Nowadays, we have colored photographs that can last forever. The first colored photographs were introduced in the early 1940s. People back then used their most modern technology called dye-coupled colors. This process connects three layers of dye s together to create the color photos we see today. However back then, they use flexible films, so this process was performed on that. In present day, when we take a picture, it is automatically colored due to the pixels in our cameras.

Types of Photography

There are many types of photography in the world. Some types are, but not limited to, nature, aerial, astrophotography, black & white, commercial, and forensic.

Nature is all about the outdoors. Photographers who take pictures of nature usually take pictures of landscapes, animals, and vegetation. Those are only some of the many things they take pictures of. Some of the world's most influential nature photographers are Galen Rowell, William Henry Jackson, Eliot Porter, and Robert Glenn Ketchum.

Ariel photography is pictures taken from planes, helicopters, and other airborne device. Also pictures of planes in-flight are also considered to be in this category. Gasper Felix Tournachon took the first photo in this category. He wanted to use his photos for map making. These first pictures were taken on a hot air balloon.

Astrophotography is pictures of space. Any pictures that include stars, planets, galaxies, and spacecraft are considered to be this category. The first picture that was space related was taken in 1939. The image was very blurry, but it lasted quite a long time.

You can obviously tell what type of photography Black & White is. Black & White photography is photos with only shades of black and white. This type of photography is used to explore shapes and texture. Shadows are very important in this photography. Ansel Adams is famous for combining nature with black & white. He is a world-renowned photographer that is worshiped all over the world.

Commercial photography is similar to commercials you see on the television. They both are trying to advertise an object. Unlike a commercial you see on television, commercial photography is still photos of the object. Riccardo Suriano is a Commercial/Advertising photographer from Rome, Italy. He started taking pictures at a very young age.

Forensic is a bit different than the rest. The police mainly use this type of photography at crime scenes. It was in the 1800s when cameras were first used for taking pictures of the crime scene.

Beien Lin

Types and Parts of a Camera

All cameras have the basic functions and parts to it. It does not matter if it is a professional camera that is a thousand dollars or a disposable camera you get from the pharmacy.

First of all, every camera should have a shutter button. This button is very important when it comes to taking pictures. The shutter button is pressed when you want to capture a moment or take a picture.

Another component of the camera would be the flash. The flash is turned on when there is not enough lighting where you take the picture. On your camera, you can choose to have the automatic flash or not. Automatic flash is when the camera sensors detect that your surrounding is too dark and turns is on for you when you press the shutter button. Some people may dislike the auto flash so they can choose to turn it off.

Another very important part of the camera would be the LCD panel. LCD represents liquid crystal display. This is the part of the camera where you can review the pictures you took. This is your little window to the outside world.

Most cameras nowadays have a USB port and a memory card slot. The main purpose of the USB port would be to import your pictures to another device for backup. The memory card slot would be needed to take pictures. All the pictures taken would be saved or file there. There are many different types of memory cards. The ones that are more expensive usually are the ones that have more memory storage.

Many expensive cameras would have the tripod socket. The tripod sockets are the place where you connect the tripod to your camera. A tripod is a stand with three legs hence the name tripod.

Most cameras nowadays can record videos. The microphone is a very important aspect when it comes to videos. The microphone captures the audio or any sound affects you want incorporated in your video. Without the microphone, movies would still be silent and you would not hear the conversations the characters are having.

The battery compartment is self-explanatory. Without the battery, the camera would not even turn on. If the camera does not urn on, how would someone even take pictures to begin with?

A well-known brand that sells high quality cameras would be Nikon. The price ranges start from around 500 dollars and exceeds 4,000 dollars. Nikon is well known as a leader in imaging products and its technology.

Another company that sells superb cameras is Canon. Canon has a large variety of products. The company's global revenue is estimated to be 36 billion dollars. The prices of these two companies are very similar. The prices start from 500 dollars to 3,000 dollars and higher.

Landscaping

Landscape pictures require time. You would need to have patience in order to take some of these shots. The lighting in all my pictures comes from the sunlight. I had to wait some time in order to get the perfect picture. Weather is also an important aspect. Make sure to check the weather before you head out. I was very lucky because the weather was very nice.

Nature

The beauty of flowers always mesmerized me. The vivid colors would always top me on my tracks. I could never resist in taking a couple of pictures while I'm at it. In order to take these pictures, you would have to personally go outside. That means you would have to get off your computers or other technical deceives and take a walk outside.

Architecture

I did take some pictures of some man made structures. Some photographers make a living by taking pictures of building and structures. For example, you go onto Google and you search up the Empire State Building. Those pictures would be considered architectural. The pictures show a man made structure or building.. These pictures can be taken rather easily. You go outside and decide to take a picture of your own house. That photograph is considered to be architectural.

Animals

I consider this category to be the toughest. Since animals can move about on their own will, you will have to match them instead. Wherever they go, you will have to follow them. Most animals dislike company, so the zoom button your camera can come in handy. You might want to get a camera with a really good zoom function if you like taking these types of photos. If you are very talented in this aspect of photography, you might even get hired by National Geographic to help them take pictures.